EARTH'S smallest SUPERHEROES

BEES

by Alix Wood

With thanks to:
Paul Hetherington
Director of Fundraising and Communications
Buglife, UK
www.buglife.org.uk

Ruby Tuesday Books

Published in 2026 by Ruby Tuesday Books Ltd.

Editors: Ruth Owen & Mark J. Sachner
Design & Production: Alix Wood

Photo credits:
Alamy: 9BR (blickwinkel), 14B (Avalon.red); Nature Picture Library: 8 (Nick Upton), 9TL (PREMAphotos), 9BL (Nick Upton), 16T (MD Kern), 18T (Ingo Arndt), 18B (Pete Oxford), 19T (Ingo Arndt), 19B (Info Arndt), 25 (Ingo Arndt); Science Photo Library: 7B (Laguna Design), 10BR (Ted Kinsman), 17BR (MD Kern), 20B (Volker Steger), 24 (Ted Kinsman); Shutterstock: Cover (Tran The Ngoc/Kuttelvaserova Stuchelova), 1 (LedyX/MagicBloods), 4T (b113), 4BL (weter78), 4BR (Kovaleva_Ka), 5TL (Shutterstock AI), 5TR (StoryTime Studio), 5BL (vallefrias), 5BR (TinasDreamworld), 6 (irin-k), 7T (Qowi Shoot), 9TR (Vinicius R. Souza), 10T (BlueRingMedia), 10BL (somchaij), 11L (Smeerjewegproducties), 11BR (Timelynx), 12–13, 14T (Sakurra), 15T (Igor Podgorny), 15C (Megan Kobe), 15BL (Andrei Dubadzel), 15BR (bikash karmokar), 16B, 17BL (Photografiero), 19C (Paul Loewen), 21 (Duda Vasilii), 22B (Rawpixel.com), 23T (MagicBloods), 23B (irin-k/SashaMagic), 26T (Kuttelvaserova Stuchelova), 26C (Pong Wira), 26B (Keith Hider), 27T (Ewelina W), 27C (Stockr), 28 (sylv1rob1/xpixel/Val_R/New Africa/Lima_84/Juergen Faelchle), 29T (Sarah Biesinger), 29CL (Valentyn Volkov), 29CR (kosolovskyy), 29B (David JC); Superstock: 11TR.

Library of Congress Control Number: 2025936190

Print (Hardback) ISBN 978-1-78856-456-4
Print (Paperback) ISBN 978-1-78856-457-1
ePub ISBN 978-1-78856-458-8

Published in Minneapolis, MN
Printed in the United States

www.rubytuesdaybooks.com

Contents

Do Superheroes Buzz?

This is a book about superheroes.
Tiny, busy, buzzing, life-saving superheroes.

Hmmm. . . .
I thought this was
a book about bees.
How can tiny insects
be superheroes?

Bees may be small, but they help make life on Earth possible.

These little insects create many of the foods we eat.

Wait a minute.
I know honeybees
make honey.
But no-one eats
THAT MUCH honey!

Along with many other types of insects, bees pollinate food crops. Birds and other types of animals do this, too.

Some scientists estimate that one-third of all the foods people eat only exist because of animal pollinators.

Bees help make this treat.

Bees help make tea and coffee.

You may not like tea or coffee. But imagine how grumpy all the adults you know would be without their morning cup!

A bee pollinating a tomato plant

No tomatoes without bees!

In fact, without bees and other pollinators, many fruits, vegetables, seeds, nuts, and edible (or cooking) oils would not exist!

And it's not just people that need plants as food. By pollinating flowers, bees help feed many other animals.

Wow. That sounds important! Perhaps bees really are superheroes. Please tell me more.

Superhero Skills and Gadgets

So if bees are superheroes, what super skills or gadgets do they have?

We're glad you asked! A bee has a whole collection of amazing built-in gadgets.

The Exoskeleton

Like all insects, bees have an external skeleton called an exoskeleton. It is made of a hard stuff called chitin.

The hairs on a bee's body are also made of hard chitin and are part of its exoskeleton.

The Wings

Bees have two pairs of wings.

A honeybee's wings can beat more than 200 times per second! It's these high-speed wing movements that make a bee's buzzing sound.

The Pollen Basket

The back legs of some bees, such as honeybees, have a built-in pouch called a pollen basket. A bee carries pollen back to its home in the basket.

The Antennae

Bees use their two antennae to smell, taste, and touch.

They can smell flowers with their antennae.

Bees don't have ears. Their antennae pick up vibrations in the air, a little like your ears do. This allows bees to hear the world around them.

The Five Eyes

Bees have two large compound eyes. They are made up of thousands of tiny lenses that create a mosaic-like view of the world.

A bee's compound eyes allow it to see almost all the way around its head—including behind. To avoid predators, the large eyes can detect movements more quickly than a human's eyes.

A bee has three smaller eyes on top of its head. These eyes detect light and help the bee navigate using the Sun.

The Mandibles

These strong jaws can be used for biting, chewing, and even construction work!

The Proboscis

This long, hairy, straw-like tongue is used for probing into flowers and sucking up nectar.

Thousands of Superheroes!

I've seen big, fuzzy bees and small, skinny bees. Are there different types?

Yes! There are more than 20,000 different species, or types, of bees. Some bees, such as honeybees and bumblebees, are social bees. They live in big groups called colonies.

Bumblebees

Bumblebee colonies have a queen and up to 400 members.

Bumblebees may build nests in trees, in compost heaps, and even in abandoned, underground mouse nests.

Because bumblebees have fat, stubby bodies and tiny wings, a scientist once claimed it was impossible for them to fly!

Bumblebees twist their wings as they fly. This means that even on the upstroke, the air around their wings is pushed downward to keep them in flight.

Most species of bees are solitary bees. These little superheroes live alone.

Leafcutter Bees

A female solitary leafcutter bee cuts pieces from leaves with her mandibles.

She uses the leaves to make package-like cells inside hollow plant stems. She lays an egg inside each cell. She puts pollen inside, too, as food for her larva, or baby.

Sweat Bees

Some types of sweat bees are solitary, while others are social.

These tiny bees get their name because they land on humans to feed on the salt in our sweat!

Mason Bees

Some female solitary mason bees make a tiny nest in a snail shell.

Scientists have cut open this mason bee's nest.

Superhero Pollinators

So bees pollinate flowers. But what exactly is pollination?

Good question! The job of a plant's flowers is to produce seeds for reproduction.

How Pollination Works

Flowers produce sweet nectar to attract hungry pollinators.

Bees can see ultraviolet light, which is a type of light that humans cannot see.

Many flowers guide bees to their nectar and pollen using ultraviolet light. The bees see special colors that are invisible to humans!

What a human sees. What a bee sees.

When a bee visits a flower to collect and feed on nectar, pollen sticks to its body. When the bee visits the next flower, some of that pollen gets brushed off.

Bees collect some pollen as food for themselves and their young.

Some bees, such as honeybees and bumblebees, use stiff hairs on their legs to collect pollen from their bodies. Then they push the pollen into their pollen baskets.

A Bee's Magnetic Superpower

A bee's body pulls pollen toward it like a magnet. How?

Have you ever created static electricity by rubbing a balloon on your hair? A bee's beating wings also create static.

Just like your hair jumping toward the balloon, pollen jumps toward the bee.

A resin bee carrying pollen on her body

Superheroes at Work

So, bees help plants reproduce. But how do they make raspberry ice cream or a cup of tea?

Many of the plants that bees pollinate are human foods. We eat the plants' leaves, flowers, fruits, or seeds.

No orange juice without bees!

Bees help pollinate many trees and other plants that produce fruits and nuts. They also help pollinate tea and coffee plants.

Tea plant flowers and leaves

No broccoli without pollinators!

Bees pollinate many vegetable plants.

Onion plant

I don't mind if we can't grow broccoli!

Bees pollinate plants that are used to make medicines.

No hamburgers without pollinators!

Oh come on. How can beef be made from flowers?

Beef comes from cows, as does milk for many types of ice cream. Cows eat grass, but farmers must also feed them plants such as alfalfa and clover that are pollinated by bees.

No sunflowers without bees!

Bees pollinate plants such as sunflowers and rapeseed that are grown to make cooking oils.

Many of the fish we eat are raised on fish farms. They are fed foods made from soya beans and other plants that are pollinated by bees.

Bees help make cotton T-shirts and jeans!

Cotton is made from soft fibers that grow inside a cotton plant's seedpods. Cotton plants can be pollinated by the wind and insects.

Plants pollinated by bees produce more cotton.

Bees also help pollinate many trees and other plants that provide food and shelter for wild animals.

Bee Super Food

All types of bees feed on nectar and pollen.

But honeybees can turn these substances into a range of incredible super foods.

Honeybees live in colonies with a queen and about 50,000 members. They naturally build hives, or nests, inside holes in tree trunks.

A honeybee has two stomachs—one for eating nectar and one for carrying nectar back to the hive.

Back at her hive, a forager bee regurgitates, or spits up, nectar to a receiver bee.

Worker bees turn the nectar into honey.

Nectar spoils if it is stored. So honeybees make long-lasting honey to feed the colony in winter, when there are no flowers.

Honey stored in a hive

Larva surrounded by royal jelly

Some worker bees mix honey, pollen, and special substances from their throats to make royal jelly. All honeybee larvae (baby bees) are fed royal jelly during their first three days of life.

The queen bee feeds on royal jelly every day!

Worker bees also mix pollen with honey and saliva to make bee bread. This nutritious food is fed to larvae and young workers.

Bee bread

How long does honey last for?

A VERY long time! It's the only foodstuff that never spoils.

Archaeologists tasted a 3,000-year-old pot of honey found in an Egyptian pyramid—it still tasted great!

Go Team Bee!

Honeybees really know how to get a job done—with teamwork!

The queen bee is the mother of the colony. She can lay up to 2,000 eggs each day—one every 43 seconds!

Workers choose some larvae to be queens. These babies are fed royal jelly every day. This special diet makes the larvae become queens with ovaries for producing eggs.

The hive's male bees are called drones. There may be just 500 drones in a hive of 50,000 bees. The males have one role—to mate with the queen.

Making a Worker Honeybee

The queen lays an egg in a brood cell made from beeswax.

A larva hatches from the egg.

The larva becomes a pupa.

The pupa becomes an adult bee, and emerges from its cell.

All the colony's worker bees are female. And each worker has her own special job to do.

The hive is at work 24 hours a day!

The Nurses

Nurse bees produce royal jelly. They feed the larvae with royal jelly and bee bread. They keep watch over the pupae and clean and repair the brood cells.

The Undertakers

Undertakers remove dead bodies from the hive. An undertaker flies with a corpse away from the hive, so it won't cause disease or attract pests.

The Attendants

These devoted servants take care of the queen day and night. They groom her and feed her royal jelly.

The House Bees

These bees keep the hive clean. They make repairs and take out the trash, such as bee poop and unwanted pollen.

The Guard Bees

Some bees guard the entrance to the hive. They keep out intruders such as wasps and robber bees from other colonies that want to steal food. The guards will sting or beat up an intruder!

The Water Foragers

Some foragers collect water for drinking and making honey. Water is also spread around the hive to help keep it cool.

The Ventilators

These bees fan their wings to ventilate, or make air flow through, the hive. Their work keeps the hive cool, moving old, warm air out and bringing cool, fresh air in.

Building Bee-Tropolis

Sometimes a honeybee colony grows too large. Then it's time to build a new bee city!

The queen leaves the hive with a swarm of thousands of bees.

Once a new home is chosen, the workers start to build.

Worker bees have glands on their abdomens that turn the sugar from honey into beeswax.

A worker collects wax from her sister.

The workers chew the wax until it is soft. Then they build circular wax cells.

The bees use their antennae and bodies to measure the size and depth of each cell they build.

Honeycombs inside a tree hole hive

Heat coming from the hard-working bees makes the cells' walls melt and flatten to make hexagons. The wax hexagons form the bees' amazing honeycombs.

Hexagon-shaped cells are strong, and there is no wasted space.

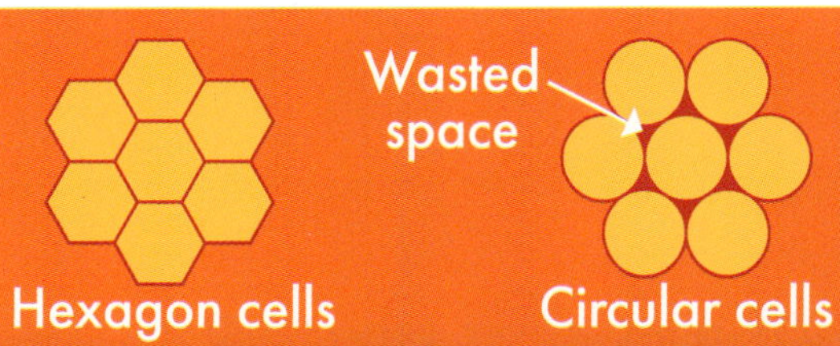

Some foragers collect resin from trees and mix it with beeswax and saliva to make propolis. This sticky disinfectant is spread around the hive and its entrance. It keeps the hive germ-free and acts like a doormat—cleaning the bees' feet as they enter!

What happens to an old hive when their queen leaves?

The bees choose a few larvae and feed them royal jelly. After about 16 days, one larva emerges as the new queen.

If several new queens emerge at once, they fight. The new queen is the bee who stings her rivals—to death!

Dancers and Navigators

It's essential that a honeybee colony finds food. Foragers use their built-in superhero features to navigate around their habitat—and share information with the team!

Bees use the Sun's position to help guide them to a good food source. Their eyes are so sensitive that bees can always tell where the Sun is—even on a cloudy day.

Bees also navigate by remembering landmarks, such as a tree stump or pond. They create a map in their brains of the area around the hive. On a foraging trip, a bee may visit up to 100 flowers.

Scientists fit trackers to honeybees to measure their foraging trips.

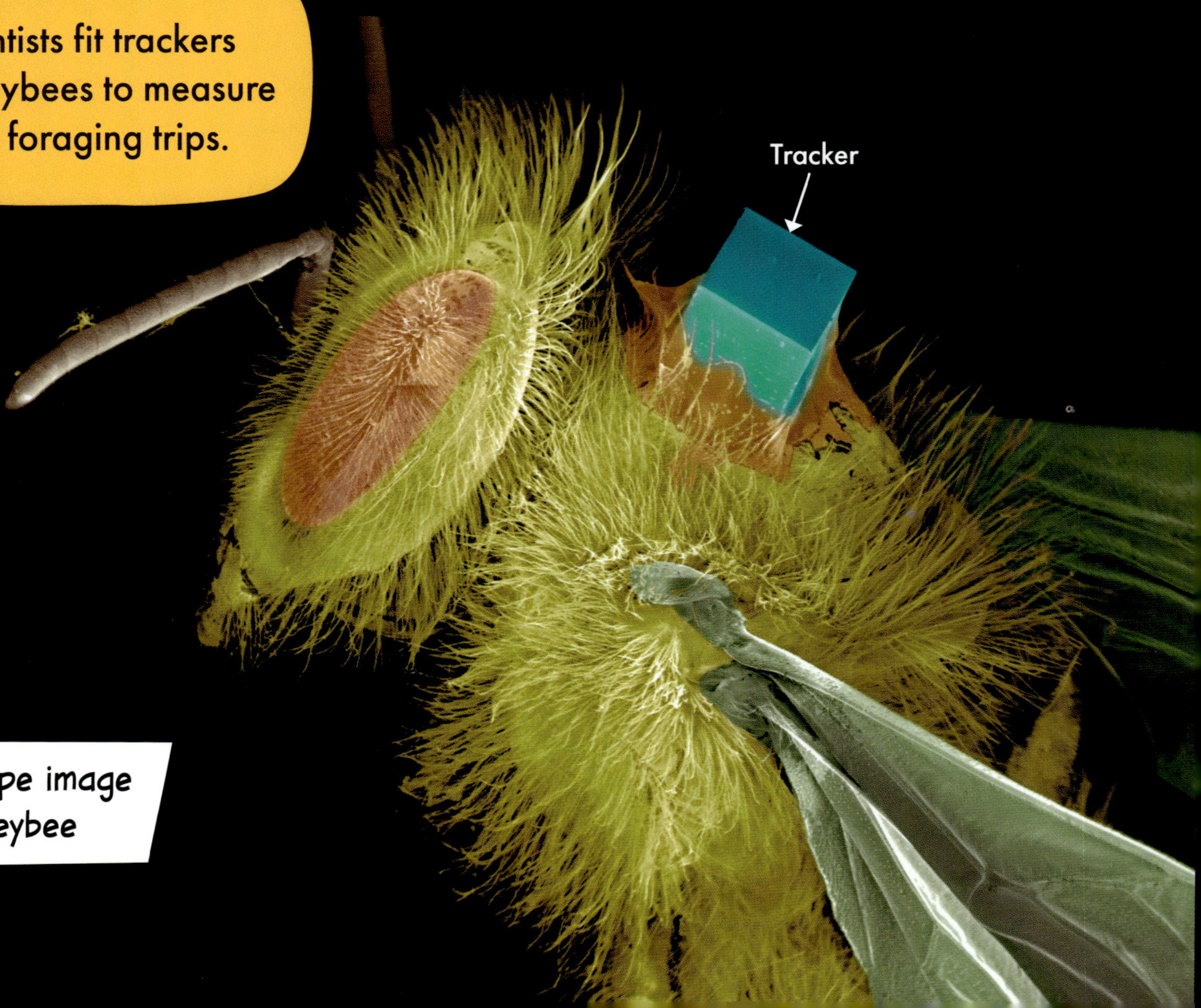

Microscope image of a honeybee

I've heard that honeybees dance. Why do they do this?

When a honeybee finds a good food source, she returns to her hive and dances to show the other foragers where to fly.

Honeybee Dance Moves

The dancing bee smells like the flower patch, and she gives her sisters a taste of the nectar. This also helps the other bees find the flowers.

If the food is farther away, the bee does a waggle dance. She waggles back and forth along a straight line. Then she circles back and repeats the waggle.

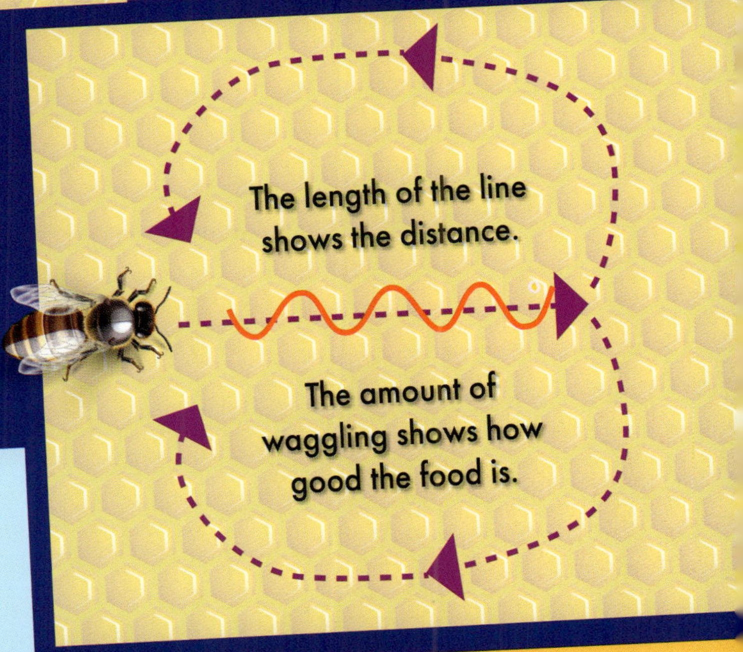

A bee may release chemical messages called pheromones close to a good flower patch. Other bees detect these smells with their antennae and head toward those plants.

Tiny Super Brains

A honeybee's brain is about the size of a sesame seed on a hamburger bun. But this tiny brain is packed with incredible power.

Marvelous Mathematicians

Bees can do math! Scientists showed bees pictures of sets of squares. Some bees were trained to recognize MORE THAN and fly to a set with more squares. Others were trained to recognize LESS THAN. The bees were rewarded with a sweet treat if they chose the right card.

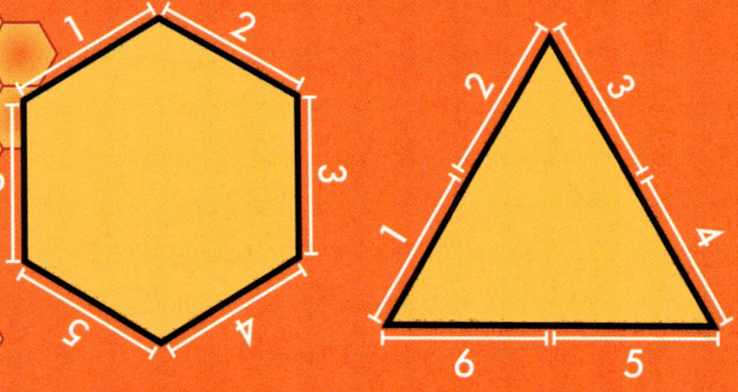

The cell walls of both shapes = 6 units

Honeybees need strong honeycombs that store as much honey as possible. Hexagon-shaped cells are strong. Triangle-shaped cells would be strong, too. Look at the two shapes. Which shape could hold the most honey? (See page 32.)

Facial Recognition

Bees can recognize human faces! Scientists gave bees some sugary liquid next to a photo of a human face. When that photo was mixed up with others, the bees remembered that face and flew to it.

Amazing Navigators

A bee must find her way home once she's loaded with nectar and pollen. Bee brains have a built-in SAT NAV that quickly and cleverly calculates the shortest route back to the hive.

Fast Learners

A honeybee begins her working life as a nurse bee. She will then do other jobs such as becoming a house bee, undertaker, or construction worker. Finally, she becomes a forager. A worker bee lives for just six weeks! In that time, she must learn a new set of skills each time she changes jobs.

Time Travelers

If a hive needs more young nurse bees, an older forager bee can go back in time. Changes happen in the bee's brain so that she becomes a young nurse bee again.

A Brain for Teamwork

A scientist trained pairs of bumblebees to push a plastic building block toward a target to receive a sweet reward. The bees figured out that they both needed to push at the same time to move the block.

Tiny but Powerful

I've heard stripes can be a warning sign. Are bees dangerous?

Tiny honeybees can pack a punch! But it's not normal for them to attack humans.

A bee's sting injects venom into its enemy. However, a worker honeybee only stings to protect herself or to defend the hive.

She uses this defense as a last resort, because it means instant death—for herself!

WARNING!
A bee sting is painful but not usually harmful. However, some people are allergic to bee stings and may need URGENT medical attention.

Part of a honeybee's abdomen seen under a microscope

A honeybee's stinger has hook-like barbs. When a honeybee stings, the stinger stays stuck in the enemy's body. As the bee flies away, part of the bee's abdomen is ripped out.

A queen honeybee's stinger is smooth. She can sting multiple times and survive.

Bumblebees and some types of solitary bees can sting many times because they have smooth stingers that don't get stuck.

Honeybees have another defensive weapon—pheromones.

If an attacker enters the hive, the bees release pheromones that say **DANGER!**

Guard bees arrive to attack the intruder. Other workers detect the pheromones and join the fight.

Honeybees forming a heat ball

The bees form a ball around the intruder.
Then they generate heat by vibrating their wing muscles.
The intense heat eventually cooks the enemy!

Every Superhero Has Enemies!

Most superheroes have enemies. How about bees?

Yes! Animals such as chimpanzees, orangutans, and badgers attack hives to eat honey, larvae, and adult bees.

Tiny mites infest honeybee hives. They live on the larvae, pupae, and adult bees—feeding on them. The mites also pass on diseases to the bees.

Orchid mantises are insects that are disguised as flowers. They hunt for bees and other pollinators.

A female beewolf grabs a bee, stings it, and paralyzes it. Then the fierce wasp carries the bee back to her underground burrow. The wasp's larvae feed on the paralyzed bee—eating it alive!

Sadly, bees have one powerful arch enemy—humans!

Habitat Destruction

People destroy forests, flower meadows, and other wild places to build roads, houses, factories, and shopping malls.

People turn plant-filled gardens into concrete-covered parking spaces.

Tractor spraying pesticides

Poisonous Pesticides

Some farmers and gardeners use chemical pesticides to kill weeds and insects that feed on plants. These pesticides kill bees!

Honeybees carry nectar that's contaminated with pesticides back to their hives. Queen bees that feed on poisoned nectar lay fewer eggs. The workers become confused and weak. They cannot find their way around or forage for their family.

Climate Change

Human-made climate change is causing forest fires and floods. These extreme events kill insects and destroy their nests.

Droughts caused by hot weather kill the plants that bees feed on.

Changing temperatures and changes to the seasons can disrupt bee life cycles.

Be Team Bee

Bees are SO awesome. What can we do to help them?

Ask for an insect hotel as a birthday or holiday gift. Bees can nest inside or stay for the winter.

Ask your family to NEVER use pesticides in your outdoor space.

Leave areas of bare soil or rough grass where ground-nesting bees can dig underground nests.

Make a pile of untreated wood where carpenter bees can lay their eggs.

Don't dig up flowering weeds, such as dandelions. Bees LOVE them!

Fill a terracotta pot with dry grass and moss, and place it upside-down in a sheltered spot. It will make a perfect winter nest for a queen bumblebee.

Grow pollen-rich, native plants, especially wildflowers, to create a bee-friendly garden.

Save a Superhero!

If you notice a bee has not moved for 45 minutes, it may be exhausted and need help.

Mix two tablespoons of white sugar with one tablespoon of water. Offer this energy drink to the bee.

Do not give a bee honey from a jar. While it's safe for us to eat, it might carry disease that's harmful to the bee.

Beekeepers raise honeybees in wooden hives and collect the honey we eat from the bees' honeycombs. In small amounts, honey is super healthy and can help our bodies fight infections and disease.

Bees are essential for our world. They pollinate trees, wildflowers, and huge numbers of food plants.

And bees are super cool. Most superheroes know they are doing good. But bees do all their work without even realizing they are helping us!

Glossary

antennae

Long body parts on the heads of insects that can be used for touching, smelling, tasting, and communication.

brood cell

In a bee's nest, a tiny, container-like space where the queen bee lays an egg. A bee goes through its larva and pupa life-cycle stages inside its brood cell.

cell

In the world of bees, a tiny, container-like space where eggs are laid. In a honeybee's hive, cells are also used for storing honey and pollen.

climate change

A change in Earth's temperature and weather that happens over a long period of time. Climate change can happen naturally, but at the moment, Earth's temperature is getting warmer primarily because of human actions.

crops

Food plants, such as wheat, oats, and tomatoes, that are grown in large quantities on farms.

exoskeleton

The tough, outer skeleton, or shell, on the body of an insect.

forager

An animal or person who looks for and gathers food.

insect

A small animal with six legs, antennae, and an exoskeleton. Most insects have wings and can fly.

larva

The young form of some animals, including insects, fish, and frogs.

lenses

The parts of eyes that focus on what an animal or person is looking at.

navigate

To figure out the best route to take from one place to another.

nectar

A sugary liquid produced by flowers.

pesticide

A substance (usually made from chemicals) that is used to kill insects, rats, weeds, or other pests.

pheromones

Scents that are released by animals as a way to communicate—for example, pheromones can be used to attract a mate or warn of danger.

pollen

A dust made by the male parts of flowers for reproduction.

pollinate

To carry pollen from the anthers (male parts) of one flower to the stigma (female part) of another, so that the second flower is fertilized and ready to make seeds.

pollinator

An insect or other animal that helps carry pollen from flower to flower.

pupa

The stage in the life cycle of some insects when the insect changes from a larva to an adult.

species

A type of living thing. The members of a species look alike and can reproduce together.

Index

Answer page 22: The outside walls of the two shapes are the same length. To measure the amount of space inside each shape, we can add small triangles. Six small triangles fit inside the hexagon. Only four will fit inside the big triangle shape. This shows a hexagon can hold much more honey. That's bee math!

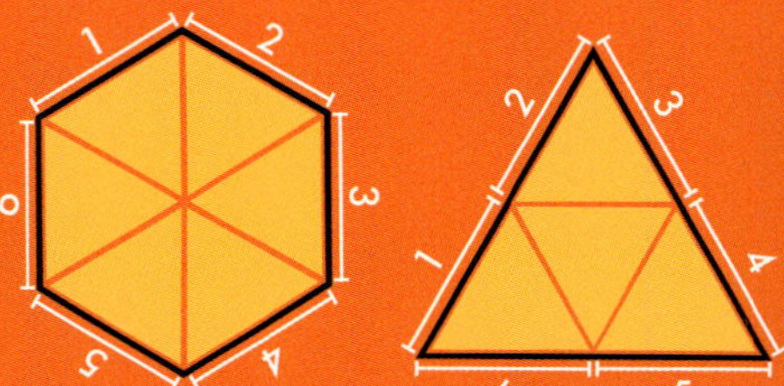